HOW TO MAKE DUTCH BABY PANCAKES

Meallá H Fallon

Content

WHAT ARE DUTCH BABY PANCAKES?

A "Dutch Baby Pancake" is basically a large pancake that gets baked in the oven (it makes a great breakfast option). The pancake batter is poured into a skillet or cake pan and then baked for 20 minutes.

You can add sweet or savory fillings, just as you wish!

This book includes instructions and recipes on how to make the Dutch Baby pancakes.

EQUIPMENT REQUIRED

Skillet (something like this one). Note it must have a handle that can go into the oven without melting!

Note:

If you don't have a skillet you can use a round cake pan (see photograph below), it works just as well.

BASIC DUTCH BABY PANCAKE RECIPE

Ingredients

2 eggs

125 ml milk

50 ml sugar

5 ml vanilla extract

125 ml flour

3 ml salt

50 ml margarine (this get used in the skillet during the baking process)

Note:

In some of the recipe variations the vanilla extract is omitted or substituted with an alternative ingredients. First check which recipe option your are making before adding this ingredient.

Method

Combine the eggs, milk, sugar and vanilla extract together.

Whisk the mixture until the eggs are light and fluffy.

Add the flour and salt.

Do not beat to much, the mixture should still be lumpy.

See Dutch Baby Variations section on the next page for the remaining part of the recipe.

Note:

The 50 ml margarine will be used during the baking process.

DUTCH BABY VARIATIONS

You can make sweet or savory Dutch Baby variations and can add many different types of fruit, nuts, chocolate, cheese or bacon..... the ideas are endless!

In the next section I will make sweet Dutch Baby pancakes.

CHOCOLATE CHIP DUTCH BABY

Additional Ingredients

187 ml chocolate chips

Icing sugar to dust the Dutch Baby pancake

Method

Add the chocolate chips to the batter (batter mixed from the basic Dutch Baby recipe).

Do not stir to stir the mixture too much, allow the mixture to remain lumpy.

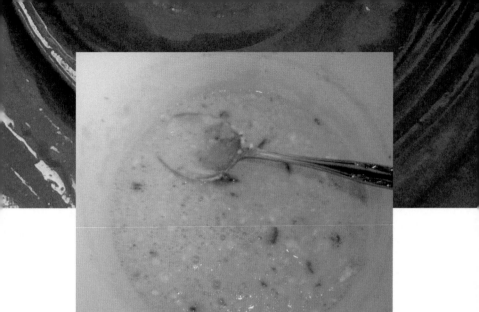

Heat the skillet or cake pan on the stove over a medium heat.

Add the 50 ml margarine to the skillet or cake pan.

Allow the butter to melt.

Remove from the heat.

Pour the batter into the hot skillet or cake pan (pour it all into the skillet or cake pan at once).

Place the skillet or cake pan into a pre-heated oven (150 degrees C).

Bake for 20 to 25 minutes.

The pancake will puff up and become golden brown.

Remove the pancake from the oven.

Sprinkle the icing sugar over the Dutch Baby.

Cut the Dutch Baby into slices.

Serve while warm, they are not as nice when cold.

APPLE CARAMEL DUTCH BABY

Additional Ingredients

250 ml cooked apple slices

Can of caramel

Method

Heat the skillet or cake pan on the stove over a medium heat.

Add the 50 ml margarine to the skillet or cake pan.

Allow the butter to melt. Remove from the heat.

Pour the batter into the hot skillet or cake pan (batter mixed from the basic Dutch Baby recipe).

Place the skillet or cake pan into a pre-heated oven (150 degrees C).

Bake for 20 to 25 minutes.

The pancake will puff up and become golden brown.

Remove the pancake from the oven.

Arrange the apple slices on top of the hot Dutch Baby.

Spoon the caramel over the apple slices.

Cut the Dutch Baby into slices. Serve while warm, they are not as nice when cold.

CHOCOLATE COFFEE DUTCH BABY

Additional Ingredients

Added To Dutch Baby Batter

10 ml coffee syrup (the type you would add to coffee or pour over ice cream)

25 ml cocoa powder

Icing For Top Of Dutch Baby

75 ml icing sugar

25 ml coffee syrup (the type you would add to coffee or pour over ice cream)

10 ml water

Method

Combine the cocoa powder and 10 ml coffee syrup together.

Mix well and make sure that there are no lumps in the mixture.

Lightly stir the cocoa mixture into the Dutch Baby batter (batter mixed from the basic Dutch Baby recipe).

Heat the skillet or cake pan on the stove over a medium heat

Add the 50 ml margarine to the skillet or cake pan.

Allow the butter to melt. Remove from the heat.

Pour the batter into the hot skillet or cake pan (pour it all into the skillet or cake pan at once)

Place the skillet or cake pan into a pre-heated oven (150 degrees C).

Bake for 20 to 25 minutes.

The pancake will puff up and become golden brown.

Remove the pancake from the oven.

Combine the icing sugar, 25 ml coffee syrup and water together.

Mix well.

Drizzle the icing over the Dutch Baby.

Cut the Dutch Baby into slices.

Serve while warm, they are not as nice when cold.

PECAN CRANBERRY DUTCH BABY

Additional Ingredients

125 ml chopped pecans

125 ml dried cranberries

Maple syrup for pouring over the Dutch Baby

Method

Add the chopped pecans and dried cranberries to the batter (batter mixed from the basic Dutch Baby recipe).

Lightly stir the batter, do not over mix the batter, it should still remain slightly lumpy.

Heat the skillet or cake pan on the stove over a medium heat

Add the 50 ml margarine to the skillet or cake pan.

Allow the butter to melt.

Remove from the heat.

Pour the batter into the hot skillet or cake pan (pour it all into the skillet or cake pan at once).

Place the skillet or cake pan into a pre-heated oven (150 degrees C).

Bake for 20 to 25 minutes.

The pancake will puff up and become golden brown.

Remove the pancake from the oven.

Cut the Dutch Baby into slices.

Drizzle the maple syrup over the Dutch Baby.

Serve while warm, they are not as nice when cold.

WALNUT FIG DUTCH BABY

Additional Ingredients

125 ml chopped walnuts

250 ml fresh figs (peeled and chopped)

Maple syrup for pouring over the Dutch Baby

Method

Add the chopped walnuts and figs to the batter (batter mixed from the basic Dutch Baby recipe).

Lightly stir the batter, do not over mix the batter, it should still remain slightly lumpy.

Heat the skillet or cake pan on the stove over a medium heat

Add the 50 ml margarine to the skillet or cake pan.

Allow the butter to melt.

Remove from the heat.

Pour the batter into the hot skillet or cake pan (pour it all into the skillet or cake pan at once).

Place the skillet or cake pan into a pre-heated oven (150 degrees C).

Bake for 20 to 25 minutes.

The pancake will puff up and become golden brown.

Remove the pancake from the oven.

Cut the Dutch Baby into slices.

Drizzle the maple syrup over the Dutch Baby.

Serve while warm, they are not as nice when cold.

APRICOT ALMOND DUTCH BABY

Additional Ingredients

125 ml slithered almonds

125 ml dried apricots (chopped)

Icing sugar to dust the Dutch Baby

Method

Add the almonds and chopped apricots to the batter (batter mixed from the basic Dutch Baby recipe).

Lightly stir the batter, do not over mix the batter, it should still remain slightly lumpy.

Heat the skillet or cake pan on the stove over a medium heat

Add the 50 ml margarine to the skillet or cake pan.

Allow the butter to melt.

Remove from the heat.

Pour the batter into the hot skillet or cake pan (pour it all into the skillet or cake pan at once).

Place the skillet or cake pan into a pre-heated oven (150 degrees C).

Bake for 20 to 25 minutes.

The pancake will puff up and become golden brown.

Remove the pancake from the oven.

Dust with icing sugar.

Cut the Dutch Baby into slices.

Serve while warm, they are not as nice when cold.

ROSE APPLE DUTCH BABY

Additional Ingredients

Substitute the vanilla extract for rose water

Few drops pink coloring

250 ml pie apples

12,5 ml rose petals

Icing sugar to dust the Dutch Baby

Method

Substitute the vanilla extract with rose water (batter mixed from the basic Dutch Baby recipe).

Add the pink food coloring, pie apples and rose petals to the batter (batter mixed from the basic Dutch Baby recipe).

Lightly stir the batter, do not over mix the batter, it should still remain slightly lumpy.

Heat the skillet or cake pan on the stove over a medium heat

Add the 50 ml margarine to the skillet or cake pan.

Allow the butter to melt.

Remove from the heat.

Pour the batter into the hot skillet or cake pan (pour it all into the skillet or cake pan at once).

Place the skillet or cake pan into a pre-heated oven (150 degrees C).

Bake for 20 to 25 minutes.

The pancake will puff up and become golden brown.

Remove the pancake from the oven.

Dust with icing sugar.

Cut the Dutch Baby into slices.

Serve while warm, they are not as nice when cold.

VANILLA LAVENDER DUTCH BABY

Additional Ingredients

5 ml lavender water

Few drops purple food coloring

25 ml dried lavender flowers

Icing sugar to dust the Dutch Baby

Method

Add the purple food coloring and lavender water to the batter (batter mixed from the basic Dutch Baby recipe).

Lightly stir the batter, do not over mix the batter, it should still remain slightly lumpy.

Heat the skillet or cake pan on the stove over a medium heat

Add the 50 ml margarine to the skillet or cake pan.

Allow the butter to melt.

Remove from the heat.

Pour the batter into the hot skillet or cake pan (pour it all into the skillet or cake pan at once).

Place the skillet or cake pan into a pre-heated oven (150 degrees C).

Bake for 20 to 25 minutes.

The pancake will puff up and become golden brown.

Remove the pancake from the oven.

Dust with icing sugar.

Cut the Dutch Baby into slices.

Serve while warm, they are not as nice when cold.

MACADAMIA, WHITE CHOCOLATE CHIP AND CHERRY DUTCH BABY

Additional Ingredients

85 ml macadamia nuts (chopped)

85 ml mini white chocolate chips

85 ml candied cherries (chopped)

Icing sugar to dust the Dutch Baby

Method

Add the chopped macadamia nuts, mini white chocolate chips and chopped candied cherries to the batter (batter mixed from the basic Dutch Baby recipe).

Lightly stir the batter, do not over mix the batter, it should still remain slightly lumpy.

Heat the skillet or cake pan on the stove over a medium heat Add the 50 ml margarine to the skillet or cake pan.

Allow the butter to melt.

Remove from the heat.

Pour the batter into the hot skillet or cake pan (pour it all into the skillet or cake pan at once).

Place the skillet or cake pan into a pre-heated oven (150 degrees C).

Bake for 20 to 25 minutes.

The pancake will puff up and become golden brown.

Remove the pancake from the oven.

Dust with icing sugar.

Cut the Dutch Baby into slices.

Serve while warm, they are not as nice when cold.

DUTCH BABY PANCAKES
SERVED WITH FRUIT

Bake the basic Dutch Baby Pancake, using the Basic Dutch Baby recipe.

Remove the Dutch Baby from oven the oven.

Cut the Dutch Baby into slices.

Serve the Dutch Baby with Fresh Fruit such as:

Strawberries (hulled)

Kiwi fruit (peeled and sliced)

Orange segments (peeled and pips removed)

Bananas (peeled, sliced and dipped in lemon juice)

Blueberries

Raspberries

Cherries

Figs

Serve with whipped cream or vanilla ice cream.

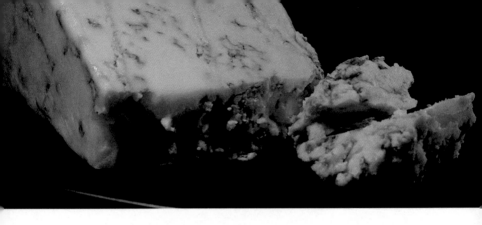

SAVORY DUTCH BABY PANCAKES

These savory Dutch Babies make delicious breakfast options!

Try these combinations:

Cheddar cheese and caramelised onion

Bacon and feta

Sundried tomato, fresh basil and feta

Bacon and maple syrup

Chorizo sausage and grated Cheddar cheese

Spring onion (green onion) and freshly ground black pepper

Spinach and feta

Ham and cheese

The combination ideas are endless......

BASIC SAVORY DUTCH BABY PANCAKE RECIPE

Ingredients

2 eggs

125 ml milk

125 ml flour

3 ml salt

50 ml margarine (this get used in the skillet during the baking process)

Method

Combine the eggs and milk together.

Whisk the mixture until the eggs are light and fluffy.

Add the flour and salt.

Do not beat to much, the mixture should still be lumpy.

Add the variation ingredients – see Savory Dutch Baby Pancake Variations below.

Lightly stir the additional ingredients into the batter.

Do not stir too much.

Heat the skillet or cake pan on the stove over a medium heat

Add the 50 ml margarine to the skillet or cake pan.

Allow the butter to melt.

Remove from the heat.

Pour the batter into the hot skillet or cake pan (pour it all into the skillet or cake pan at once).

Place the skillet or cake pan into a pre-heated oven (150 degrees C).

Bake for 20 to 25 minutes.

The pancake will puff up and become golden brown.

Remove the Dutch Baby from the oven.

Cut the Dutch Baby into pieces.

Serve warm.

SAVORY DUTCH BABY PANCAKE VARIATIONS

Try these savory Dutch Pancakes for breakfast or brunch or even just a delicious tea time snack!

Cheddar And Caramelised Onion Dutch Baby

Ingredients To Be Added To Basic Savory Dutch Baby Batter

125 ml grated Cheddar cheese

125 ml caramelized onion

5 ml freshly ground black pepper

Method To Make The Caramelized Onion

2 red onions (peeled and chopped)

12,5 ml olive oil

Sauté the red onion and olive oil together for at least 15 minutes.

Remove from the heat once the onion is soft and transparent.

Bacon And Feta Dutch Baby

Ingredients To Be Added To Basic Savory Dutch Baby Batter

125 ml crumbed feta

125 ml diced, fried bacon

5 ml freshly ground black pepper

Sundried Tomato, Basil And Feta Dutch Baby

Ingredients To Be Added To Basic Savory Dutch Baby Batter

125 ml sundried tomatoes (chopped into smaller pieces)

125 ml feta (crumbled)

12,5 ml fresh basil leaves (chopped)

5 ml freshly ground black pepper

Bacon And Maple Syrup Dutch Baby

Ingredients To Be Added To Basic Savory Dutch Baby Batter

250 ml diced, fried bacon

Maple syrup

Method

Mix the bacon into the Savory Dutch Baby batter.

Drizzle the maple syrup over baked Dutch baby just before serving.

Corn And Cheese Dutch Baby

Ingredients To Be Added To Basic Savory Dutch Baby Batter

125 ml grated Cheddar cheese

125 ml hole corn kernels (cooked)

Chorizo Sausage And Cheddar Cheese Dutch Baby

Ingredients To Be Added To Basic Savory Dutch Baby Batter

250 ml Chorizo sausage (thinly sliced)

125 ml grated Cheddar cheese

5 ml freshly ground black pepper

Spinach And Feta Dutch Baby

Ingredients To Be Added To Basic Savory Dutch Baby Batter

250 ml spinach (chopped and blanched in boiling water)

125 ml crumbled feta

5 ml freshly ground black pepper

Ham And Cheese Dutch Baby

Ingredients To Be Added To Basic Savory Dutch Baby Batter

125 ml diced, cooked ham

125 ml grated Cheddar cheese

Spring Onion (Green Onion) And Black Pepper

Ingredients To Be Added To Basic Savory Dutch Baby Batter

20 ml spring (green) onions (peeled and diced)

5 ml freshly ground black pepper

Made in the USA
Middletown, DE
29 June 2023